a to Z

Interior Decoration
a to Z

BETTY PEPIS

DOUBLEDAY & COMPANY, INC.
GARDEN CITY, NEW YORK

By the same author

BOOKS IN YOUR HOME
BETTY PEPIS' GUIDE TO INTERIOR DECORATION
HOUSE AND GARDEN GUIDE TO INTERIOR DECORATION
BE YOUR OWN DECORATOR
LE GUIDE PRATIQUE DE LA DECORATION
THE PERSONAL TOUCH IN INTERIOR DECORATING

All color is from NEW IDEAS FOR
DECORATING except for the following:
Page 1 – courtesy Beadangles; *Pages 5, 88* –
courtesy Bigelow-Sanford Carpet Co.; *Page 49* –
courtesy Nettlecreek Industries; *Pages 56, 59,
62, 81* – courtesy Du Pont Textile Fibers.

Interior decoration is the mid-twentieth century's contribution to the arts of living. For only in our own time has the planning, placement, and selection of furnishings been dignified by being deemed a profession.

Indeed the oldest professional organization of decorators in the United States (who today prefer to be called designers in the belief that this latter word is more all-encompassing) dates back to 1931. And Elsie de Wolfe, later Lady Mendl, who, perhaps somewhat inaccurately, has been called the first interior decorator, turned to this vocation around the turn of the century and did her most important work in the years just preceding 1920.

Prior to this period and to a certain extent even up to the 1930s, decorating, per se, was for the rich who relied for help, guidance, and instruction upon architects or a superior breed of craftsmen: cabinet-makers of the caliber of Chippendale and Hepplewhite in England and in our own country, Duncan Phyfe.

Men such as these set fashions, created a certain over-all look. But it was not one to which the average householder could aspire. The style—oriented furniture store and decorating sections of department stores, both catering to the many rather than the few, are of reasonably recent vintage and it is these along with the growing number of individual decorators who have evolved the pattern of making fashion important in the home.

In line with this development a whole new vocabulary has come into being. Because practitioners of this very contemporary profession compile as well as create, words have been borrowed from adjacent arts (painting and architecture, to name only two) and given new application and meanings. Other words and phrases have been manufactured to suit situations peculiar to modern residential design. Open floor plan is one example. Room divider and clerestory are others.

Modern technology and engineering have contributed too. Cantilevered chests and molded chairs are among contemporary additions to the elements of interior design—and not in name only but in concept as well.

Probing the past for inspiration has resulted in the excavation of terms that were for a time out of use, and had lost meaning for the average amateur, who, ten years ago, might not have known or cared what the difference was between an epergne and an *étagère*, or between a galloon and a gadroon. Today, all four might pertain to the furnishings of a simple living room.

Increased travel and more intensive international communication have lead to broader knowledge and acceptance of arts and crafts from various parts of the world. As a result, rya rugs share space with sliding shogi, and though neither word has been widely known, both are frequently applied to room designs today.

The well-dressed room has become a status symbol denoting knowledge-ability and sophistication, outranking in importance, at the moment, even the compact foreign car. As such, it invites analysis in somewhat abstract terms, and each of the taste-making authors has come up with his or her own newly coined definition of, for example, elegance.

This book is designed as a visual guide through the maze of words from many sources that make up the vocabulary of modern interior design. A perusal of it will inevitably result in recognition of the trends of the times (a much more complex matter than at any period of the past), for the words simply define the increasingly varied elements that contribute to contemporary decoration.

Accessories. Machine-made objects and many imports supplement hand-crafted accents in rooms of today. Among their more notable contributions is the vivid, smashing color they can add. Strikingly brilliant examples are the red lacquer table, orange glass bowl at left. Imports also add a special flavor; included here are a gilded bird from Burma, a delicate screen from Japan, and lacquer boxes from that country, a Danish red glass cylinder performing as a lamp base, an old Chinese lacquered leather box, Moroccan lantern wrought of brass and stained glass. Accessories, because they are small, can be blatant in color and quite exotic in flavor for greater impact.

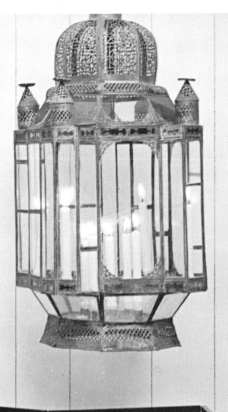

Accessories. Large pieces of colored furniture are among the most popular of these in use today and may be found in all of the period styles as well as the contemporary versions like the vitrine, tall chest, and small three-legged table seen here. Colonial chairs with mustard or slate-blue frames, French *bergères,* pastel-tinted, and with upholstery to match the watery blues, pale greens and apricots, stark modern cube tables in primary tones of red, yellow, or blue are other devices that can add excitement to decorating a room.

Accessories. Accouterments for dining are included among these and serve a most important purpose in brightening the home. They are more colorful than ever before in history: printed cloths, harmonizing napkins, platters, and plates that pick up a room's scheme all add up to a dashing informality that is in line with today's casual living and is a far cry from the stiff damasks, tall stemware, and decorated plates once popular.

Accessories. Serving pieces should not be overlooked when assembling the essentials of decorating. Emphasis on home entertaining makes these an important part of decoration, and selection should conform with all the other elements of decoration. Outdoor events, as well as indoor ones, deserve consideration. Release from the onetime binding conventions has made it possible, in recent years, to exert as much play of imagination in choosing these as in picking out any other type of accessory for decorating.

ADAM STYLE. Style devised by two English architects (brothers) in the late eighteenth century. Furniture designed by them has a certain delicacy, is much infused with the classicism of Rome, is often painted or veneered in unusual woods (satinwood, for example). Table here is typical.

ADAPTATION. Furniture that captures the spirit of a period without exactly duplicating the precise measurements or motifs. The dining room table and chairs at right are based on originals found in Williamsburg, Virginia and dating from the eighteenth century. Dimensions are smaller.

ALCOVE. Small room off of a larger one. Most often put to use to contain a bed. Today, a much used device to conceal sleeping quarters during daytime hours, but can also be effectively adapted as a book-lined study area.

AMERICANA. The folk-art of our American forefathers is so called. Includes such whimsies as weathervanes and shop signs as well as paintings, prints, carved wood figures.

ANTIQUE. Anything old, old according to the United States Customs Office being an object made before 1830. Applies to made-in-America furnishings and art like that shown here or importations from abroad including accessories.

ANCIENT. Considerably older than antique, dating in actuality to antiquity like this Islamic jar, which was made in the seventh or eighth century. A Greek urn, an Egyptian figurine also fit in this category.

(COURTESY MUSEUM OF MODERN ART)

APPLIQUÉ. A decoration that is applied to another surface. It can be three-dimensional such as a sconce or wall clock or lacquer added to metal, or refer to cutouts of one fabric sewn on top of another.

APRON. One way to dress up a battered tabletop—preferably a round one such as that at left. Mostly made of stiff fabrics like taffeta or velvet and always with a floor-length hem. More technically, an apron is a piece of wood set at right angles to the underside of a table as illustrated below.

ARCHITECTURAL DETAIL. Those additions to box-like rooms which give some distinction to the pared-down simplicity of so many homes and apartments of today. Although they appear to be of structural significance, they are purely decorative, not functional. The moldings here are one example. Other types follow.

Architectural detail can be painted on, following earlier traditions of France and Italy. Even the ceiling has been so treated in the dining room at left which one approaches through doors painted to simulate marble. This treatment is more appropriate in a traditional than a modern room. Not-so-classical columns were architectural detail added to the room at right. They seem to support the arches above the windows, although they do no such thing. They do, however, serve to give importance to the window bay and create a frame for a spectacular view.

ARMOIRE. Tall cabinet with doors, meant for hanging clothes. Can supplement closets when there are too few. Modern interpretations are showing up.

ARTIFACT. Article of great age, made by man in an earlier civilization. Valued for its antiquity. These Peruvian pots supported on brackets are typical.

ART MODERNE. Style that flourished in France during the 1920s, then put in a brief appearance in the United States. Much under the influence of cubist painting as seen in the rug at left.

ART NOUVEAU. Protest movement that broke away from the precedents of past periods and reached out for new expressions in decoration. The florid floral above shows the preference for a swirling line also illustrated in the interior at right. Established around 1900 and popular again.

(COURTESY MUSEUM OF MODERN ART)

25

ART WALL. The current craze for collecting art, often much of it minor, has led to the development of this taste for massing many pictures in a single composition on a wall. The impact they can have when presented in such formation can be as dramatic as that of a single stunning masterpiece of a large size. The advantage of this approach: it permits the inclusion of artworks not strong enough to stand on their own, and a mixture of many types of media is possible. Four examples are shown here.

ARTS AND CRAFTS. Often used to soften the severe, strict lines of modern furniture, these hand-fabricated objects may be made of many materials: of pottery, of woven reeds, of twisted wire as seen above. On occasion, they are useful, as is the perforated ceramic lantern below; at other times—simply meant for decorative effect.

ASYMMETRIC. Kind of arrangement
that achieves a sense of balance
through the use of harmonizing sizes
and styles rather than matched pairs of
tables, chairs, or lamps. A good example is
the living room above in which the
principle is accentuated by the off-center
placement of the coffee table balanced
by a pile of pillows. Such a carefully
composed setting seems more pleasing in
modern rooms than stiff regimentation.

AVANT-GARDE. Style of decoration that disregards the precedents of the past; forecasts for the future. The startling setting, left, is a case in point. The living room of a well-known architect, it is an experimental study in the use of plastics. Sheets of white plastic sheath the walls, are used for tabletops supported by slabs of clear plastic. Eventually these far-out ideas can find acceptance. The concept of cushions on a platform for seating seemed daring in 1952 (top right). Today it has become a favored fashion. See the two rooms, right.

b

AUTHENTIC. Either the original antique or a precise copy of it. In the case of this chair, both exist. The prototype, now in a museum in Paris, celebrated the balloon ascension of the Montgolfiers.

BALUSTER. An upright member, often in an elongated urn shape as above, used to support a handrail. Commonly used as an accompaniment to stairs but equally effective as a device to define and mark off a section of a room.

BAMBOO. Not necessarily made from the actual branches of this tropical plant are the many handsome chairs one sees. Imitations in wood of these shapely stalks, popular ever since the eighteenth century, unlike the real thing won't warp or split in steam-heated rooms.

BAROQUE. Large scale, bold detail, and sweeping curvilinear lines are characteristic of this style, which originated in Italy in the sixteenth century. Despite its fascination, it has little application today because of these decidedly imperious qualities.

BANQUETTE. Seating setup built in along a wall and specifically planned for use while eating. A way to achieve an air of both opulence and intimacy in even the tiniest dining area. The mural, here, draped like a window, adds glamor.

BASKETS. Objects woven of reeds, handmade around the world, have acquired acceptance as proper appurtenances for the home. Sometimes they make surprising switches: a fish basket, for example, converts to a lamp and a storage trunk turns up as a coffee table.

BEADS. These many splendored bits of cork, wood, crystal, and now even plastic, add drama to doorways or windows, can be hung from the ceiling to serve as room dividers. Used in the Near and Far East for centuries, they add a subtly exotic touch to a modern room.

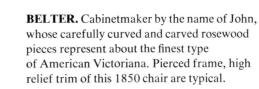

BELTER. Cabinetmaker by the name of John, whose carefully curved and carved rosewood pieces represent about the finest type of American Victoriana. Pierced frame, high relief trim of this 1850 chair are typical.

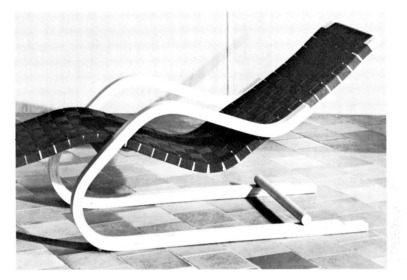

BENTWOOD. Bending wood was a technique developed in late nineteenth-century Europe. It streamlined both the manufacture of chair design (as in the frame, here, made of only two pieces of wood), and the basic design.

BERGÈRE. Actually the French word for a shepherdess, but applied to armchairs in various French styles designed to accommodate the exaggerated side-paneled skirts of these rural ladies. Inside of arm is upholstered.

BIBELOT. More than a trinket, more than a toy (the two conventional definitions). Proof of the statement that good things come in small packages, perfume bottles and miniature boxes are among these collector's items.

BIEDERMEIER. Furniture style named after a cartoon figure in mid-eighteenth-century Vienna. A little plump, a little pompous, but amply endowed with the famed Viennese charm, it can be updated as seen below.

BOMBÉ. Shape of a chest which bulges out lusciously in the center front and makes secondary small dips at the sides. Characteristic of sophisticated Parisian chests of the time of Louis XV—and also Provincial.

BRUTAL. Not derogatory as one might expect but simply descriptive of a kind of architectural (and interior) design that esteems the use of natural unpolished materials such as in this stony, cave-like room.

CABRIOLE. A well-turned leg with rounded knee typical of eighteenth-century American and English design. Low ones held lowboys, high ones held highboys, and medium ones are found on chairs.

CANE. The decorating application of this is to sit upon rather than to walk with. The basic material—a sturdy reed—is the same, but it is woven in an airy open-work design as these seats, backs.

BUNCHING. Custom of lining box-like furniture of the same size and shape but with different fittings (doors, shelves, drawers) along a wall so they appear built-in. A twentieth-century development.

CAMPAIGN FURNITURE. Portable, collapsible furniture of a type contrived for Napoleon's officers on their marches. Chests come apart, chairs fold up as do bedsteads. Translated into modern forms like those illustrated here: good for families on the move.

CANOPY. Drapery suspended over any piece of furniture. Could be a sofa, but more often is a bed, where its original purpose was to provide protection against both enemies and drafts. Although both objectives appear to be obsolete, decorative values remain.

CERAMIC. Clay contributes many varied ingredients to the arts of decoration. Combine earth with fire and you can come up with ordinary brick, old or new, or a handsomely textured wall (left). The same ingredients handled differently will produce delicate hand-crafted bowls. Three more applications are included in the room at right: a shiny white tiled floor, a tabletop of multicolored squares and hanging lanterns pierced and finished with flower-like designs. Because of their alliance with the earth, all work very well out-of-doors.

CLERESTORY. Term borrowed from church architecture to describe windows placed high on the wall of a building, permitting both light and ventilation to enter without breaking into the lower portion of the wall. A frequently seen design technique in contemporary homes where these under-ceiling strips of window often face whole walls of glass.

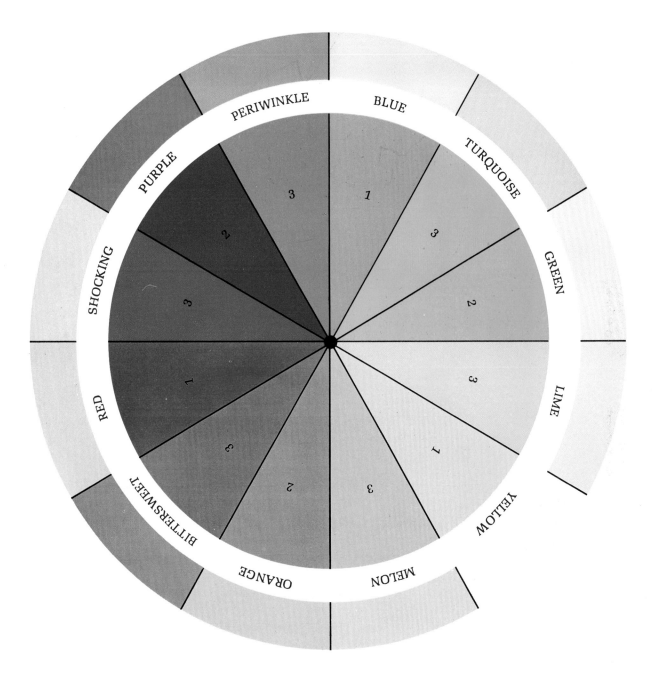

COLOR. The most inexpensive asset in all of decorating. The color wheel, above, a rainbow in circular form, is the basis of good color planning, shows the relationship of one color to another. It provides the clue to four basic schemes described in the following pages. They are called by name: monochromatic, analagous, complementary, and triadic.

Color. Clues for color schemes derive from a great range of inspirations, can come from a painting, a printed fabric, or more unexpectedly, from a piece of furniture such as the small round Venetian chest below which suggested the pastel scheme ranging from pale to vivid. From the floral painting on its façade were chosen the greens, golds, and intense corals of the fabrics and accessories, all underlined by earth tones of the rya rug.

Fan-shaped vase of Tiffany glassware, below, has the
brilliant peacock-feather hues, encouraged the creation of
a daring and off-beat scheme, its richness emphasized
by the inclusion of golden brass accents. The stained glass
tones are given further definition by the addition of
touches of fuchsia and the jolting surprise note of the
turquoise blue hexagonal floor tiles. A lacquered screen or
box could start another scheme.

Color. Monochromatic schemes, based on the color wheel, are composed of tints and shades of a single color. Because of their simplicity, they are highly sophisticated. And because there is little color variation (black and white and neutrals do not count), variation of texture becomes all important to avoid monotony. Using them takes semi-professional skill. Any of the twelve colors shown on the wheel may be handled in such fashion. Dull tones such as the deepened golds, left, or bright ones such as the corals below lend themselves equally well to this kind of treatment. Touches of white in both cases leaven the effect of undiminished, undiluted color.

Color. Analagous schemes make use of colors that are side by side on the color wheel on page 49. They have become the rage in recent years, making use as they do of modern-looking, color-clashing tones. They can give a contemporary lift to traditional rooms, and because the guide lines are so positive, are easy to work out. Orange walls keynote the brilliant color planning conceived here. Surrounding it on the color wheel are the sharp hues of the orange-red covering on some of the furniture, golden tones on others.
A combination of blues, greens, lavenders is a variant of the analagous approach to color in decorating an interior.

Color. Complementary schemes are sharp and decisive, make avant-garde rooms look even more so, and give an up-to-date appearance to settings, such as that at left, in which primarily period pieces are used. To compose one, refer again to the color wheel and choose colors exactly opposite. In these two cases the contrast is afforded by pairing red with yellow-green. Purple and yellow, green and red are other examples of complementary schemes which should always be confined to two colors.

Color. Triadic schemes relate well to conventional, traditionally inspired furnishings, are based, as the name implies, on three colors (often considered the maximum that should be used in a single room). To pick them correctly use the color wheel again and settle for all of the primary colors (labeled 1) or secondary or tertiaries, all numbered accordingly. The simplest of all triadic schemes: red, yellow, and blue has been selected in the case of both the contemporary settings here. Paler tones of the same shades would work very effectively in rooms that are more closely linked to tradition.

Color. Neutral schemes do not depend upon the color wheel but make use of what are known as the "no-color" colors: beiges and grays, taupes and browns, off-whites and gunmetals. Interesting textures: straw-like materials, strong wood grains, woven fabrics with a tweedy look, floor coverings with a sense of depth, are essential to avoid monotony. Backgrounds such as these are the perfect foil for modern paintings with decisive color, accessories with more than the usual amount of brilliance (piles of clashing pillows, for example), and the brightly colored backs of books. Restful and serene, they are endowed with a certain amount of urbanity that makes them seem most comfortably at home with furnishings which are very much of today or under a Japanese influence.

Color. Creams and ivory, oyster and bone and all of the other off-white tones have recently earned their place as basic colors for a room's scheme. Made possible— and even practical—by the introduction of new finishes on fabrics and easy-to-maintain combinations of fibers for floor coverings, such schemes have a luxurious look that makes them extremely stylish.

Then, too, the simplicity of an off-white
scheme makes permissible the use of
reasonably ornate furniture and
accessories, setting these apart like jewels.
As with other neutral color plans, white
schemes also invite the injection of
artwork of unusually strong character.
As far as period goes, however, as the
two settings here indicate, white is
equally at home with traditional or modern.

Color. White with a single brilliantly sharp color added is another color approach increasing in popularity. It is easy to formulate, and its striking effectiveness can do much to distract from and rejuvenate tired furnishings.

CONVERSATION PIT. A
seating group that is dropped
below the regular floor level of
the rest of the room. Offers
a sense of seclusion for those
occupying the sofa units
that are invariably built
right into this pit.

COROMANDEL. A dark
wood, found in the Far East,
where it is used for furniture—
very often lacquered. Most
memorable of all are the tall,
dark, and handsome screens
with intricately detailed
scenes. Rare, rich in color and
detail, such a screen dominates
and dramatizes almost
any setting.

CORNICE. The top finish or crowning glory of a piece of furniture or even the front of a building. Or, as above, reiterating a usage of the eighteenth century: an extended box which conceals curtain and drapery rods. It can also cover bulbs for indirect lighting.

CORNY. Embarrassingly unsophisticated. Results from too dedicated a devotion to reproducing down to the last itsy-bitsy detail the interiors of our colonial ancestors—forgetting that, in every period, people do depart from overly precise patterns of their own time.

Floor Coverings. Mellow tones of old orientals
are much appreciated for their subtly aged quality
which glows when combined with contemporary
colors and furnishings. When, as here, a precious rug
supplies the only pattern in the room, its importance
and value are emphasized. Antique rugs from
other areas of the world: fuzzy neutrals tinged with
orange from Morocco, pale pastels fabricated
at Aubusson in France with a flat needlepoint
technique, and muted colored, carved temple rugs of
old China are equally prized for the distinction
they can give a room. When the floor covering
becomes that important it can contribute, as it has
here, the theme for the color scheming of a room.
On priceless examples as much of the pattern
as possible should be permitted to show and left
completely free of furniture pieces.

Floor Coverings. Sharp shades of modern patterned rugs
can provide a vivid exclamation point of interest in a room.
Whether worked with a thick-piled, flat surface as at left
or fuzzy, long-haired technique as below, they are best suited
for use in small areas where they may provide a focal point
for a grouping of furniture. It is permissible to place them on
top of plain carpets, or as is more usually done, on a
hard-surfaced floor whether of wood or some other material.
Strictly a twentieth-century addition to the vocabulary
of design, they share one thing in common with patterned rugs
of the past: where the design is strong, it should be permitted
to be the dominant, if not the only pattern in any room
where used. These are called either accent or area rugs.

Floor Coverings. Hard surfaces, whether man-made (left)
or of natural materials (the slate, above) play an increasingly
interesting role in interior decoration. Among the more
intriguing developments of recent years have been vinyl tiles,
printed, plain, in bright colors and clear ones and ofttimes
imitating almost to perfection the work of nature. Travertine
tiles of this plastic, like those used at the left, must be touched
to distinguish them from the real thing. The increasing
trend toward leaving much of a floor bare has focused interest
on floors of this type. Real marble, glass mosaic, and
wood parquet are now also making a comeback.

Floor Coverings. Textures of many types are another device used to call attention to floors. The shaggy look of a rug such as this one is an example. Others have carved borders and designs cut into two or even three depths of the pile. They are, however, noticeably less demanding than patterned rugs of any vintage, old or new.

FOLK ART. Crafts identified with unsophisticated cultures but sufficiently interesting to warrant inclusion in a decorating plan. Seen above: bed-covering and rug from our own Southwest; wall hanging from South Seas.

FORMAL. Decorating plan arrived at with quiet precision, luxurious materials. For success, demands superb housekeeping with everything in place. Tinged with tradition rather than contemporary casualness.

h

HALL CLOCK. Alternate for grandfather clock, applies to any tall timepiece encased in a cabinet. Modern designs are joining the ranks of traditional period pieces.

GRILLE. Openwork metal or wood grating used at a door or window and, today, also employed as a room divider because it makes possible a very subtle sense of separation.

GUNMETAL. Alloy of which cannons were made. Worked into accessories during the seventeenth century when its dull, tarnished look was liked.

HEPPI
workin
century
delicate
earlier

HIBAC
by Japa
food. M
origina
hors d'

INTERNA
appreciated
modern ap
work of mo
materials f
and glass) i
to contemp
supplemen
interfere w

HANGING SHELVES. Cliché of the contemporary decorating scene. These shelves which serve as a catch-all for controlled clutter may well go down in history as the hallmark of mid-twentieth-century rooms. On them, books share space with souvenirs, art objects play a part as well as plants. They are the focal point of many modern rooms.

INDIAN. M[...]
cultures con[...]
to present-d[...]
Intricately w[...]
shot cloth; st[...]
of brass are [...]
and rewardi[...]
found in mo[...]

INDIVIDU[...]
admired and [...]
that can be a[...]
decoration, f[...]
exertion of a[...]
personal tast[...]
can be no sug[...]
Expressed w[...]
at right.

MESH. Twentieth-century material engineered to give resiliency and bounce to a chair by replacing conventional upholstery with shaped steel cushioning. Impervious to weather it is ideally suited to outdoor use.

MIES CHAIR. Classic of all modern chairs, it was designed by an architect, Mies van der Rohe, and originally exhibited in Barcelona, Spain, in 1927. It is still being made in the United States and is esteemed by modernists as one of the great designs of all time. It is chrome and leather.

(COURTESY MUSEUM OF MODER[...]

MOBILE. Abstract sculpture that moves when touched by a breeze or the human hand. It may dangle from the ceiling, as this one does, or hang on a post. "Invented" by the artist Alexander Calder in the 1930s, the principle has been both imitated and enlarged upon.

MODERN. Style of decorating peculiar to the mid-twentieth century. It does not exclude pieces from the past but manages to give old things a new look by placing them in proximity to more modern designs and arrangements as in this corner conversation area where antique stools cluster around a contemporary coffee table. This forthright mixing of periods is very characteristic.

Modern. Restraint and a rejection of fussiness distinguishes this present-day fashion in decor. Plain carpeting, plain painted walls, simple pull-back draperies keep the handsome French pieces in the room at right from seeming overwhelmingly formal. Addition of modern art: painting over the desk, metal sculpture on the coffee table are other elements that designate this as a room of today rather than from some earlier era. Bookshelves built-in along a facing wall and revealed only in the reflection of the large mirror over the sofa contribute further to a completely contemporary impression despite the emphasis on the French period furniture.

Modern. The revolution in color which took place in the 1950s is partially what gives a modern look to American interiors. Conservatism and caution have gone down the drain, and present-day interiors take on a brilliance never seen in any country before. This freedom to use strong straight color (a true red, an intense blue, an undiluted yellow) is unprecedented in the history of interior decoration and therefore correctly referred to as "modern." This attitude will unquestionably continue to characterize color attitudes of the future, whether in rooms fitted out with period or contemporary pieces.

Modern. Furniture that looks built-in, taking on an architectural flavor is part of the modern approach to decorating. Shelves, whether single ones or a wall of them, may go down in history as an identifying mark of our own particular period. What goes on the shelves is also pretty typical, for books rarely stand alone but share space with propped pictures, collector's items, simple souvenirs and curios. This trend offers an unparalleled opportunity to achieve that most valued quality in interior decorating: a highly individual and personal touch. The impact these shelf arrangements have makes them dominate the whole room.

Modern. Fitting closed storage and concealed sound equipment into a wall of shelves is an extension of the comparatively recent concept explored on the preceding pages. Although the general effect is of a custom-made, specially planned wall, this particular example, like many others, was made up from ready-made units.

MOLDED CHAIR. Chair based on a frame that is molded or pressed into shape rather than, as in former ages, glued and nailed. Most are pleasingly sculptural.

MODULE. Standard measurement—applicable to architecture, and now to furniture design. Makes it possible to fit chests together to make them appear built-in.

(COURTESY MUSEUM OF MODERN ART)

MONDRIAN. Twentieth-century painter whose asymmetric compositions of black lines and bright blocks of red, yellow, and blue on a white ground have had a profound effect on interior design, suggesting fabrics and furniture arrangement, as well as actual duplication, seen here, on a kitchen wall.

Pattern Placement. Applied to a large piece of furniture, a sofa, for example, a print can accomplish one of two purposes. It can suggest a whole new color scheme for a room, or, if carefully selected, can act as a catalyst blending together the already existing elements. In either event it should be bold, positive, and with a clearly defined color scheme. In this case, lavender and blue blossoms suggested the fabric on the easy chairs which combine the two shades in an almost unnoticeable stripe. The yellow-green of the French *bergères* also shows up faintly in the pattern. The rug, a tweed, combines all of the colors. Stripes and tweedy types of textiles are non-competitive to more distinct and more illustrative patterns, and work effectively with them.

146

Pattern Placement. Brilliant
of the bedroom, left, dictate
scheme of blues and purple
Matching quilted spread an
the palest tones, while the r
three chairs—each of them
these disparate elements.

Wall covering on a large s
one-room apartment, con
suggesting red for vitrine,
repetition of design on the
Geometric nature of brai
covers (the only other pat
not compete with stylized

SKYLIGHT. Window cut into a ceiling to permit light to filter down from the sky above. In modern houses may be fitted with a plastic bubble which can also be illuminated after dark. At left, plain glass was used.

SPACE PLANNING. Considering all of the architectural assets and deficits as well as the furnishings when decorating. In this tiny room, windows, walls, and ceiling are very important to the over-all effect.

SPACE SAVING. Kind of multi-purpose, double-duty furniture that by performing more than one function leaves room for other essentials. It might be a desk that doubles for dining or a table that expands.

SPANISH. Strong influence on decorating trends of the 1960s, this extremely ornate style affected the look of backgrounds: encouraging the use of tiles on floors and walls and the introduction of carved and metal grilles. Heavy furniture, carved, inlayed, or combined with black iron and brilliant patterned rugs and spreads, are other aspects of this particular trend.

STACKING. Pieces planned to fit one on top of another for condensed storage. Cups and saucers, pitchers and platters and even chairs are formulated in this fashion today.

STORAGE WALL. Built-in cabinets, drawers, desks, and even beds occupying most or all of a wall and designed to care for an individual's (or a family's) possessions.

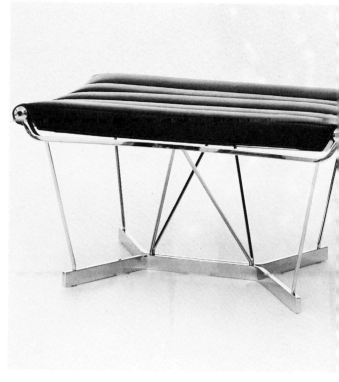

STRAW. Dried stalks of grain, the earliest type of bedding when shredded and strewn on the floor. More intricate treatments wind up as stools for indoors—or outdoors.

STRUT. Bar that by exerting pressure holds up a bridge, or, in this case, a stool. Engineering principle applied to furniture design results in a slick, industrial look.

STUDIED. Rigid, carefully planned placement that leaves little or no room for a change. The boxes on this open table have, for example, been worked into a composition.

STYLIZED. Motifs that express the essential form rather than the realistic appearance of that which inspired the pattern, as the tulips here that never grew in any garden.

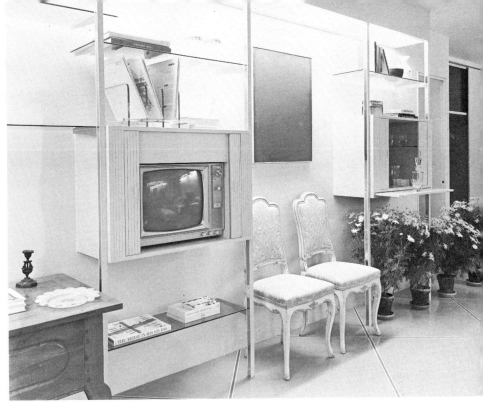

SUNDIAL. Time-telling gadget that ticks off the daytime hours by casting a shadow on a flat plate or cylindrical surface.

SUSPENDED. Floating state of furniture that is free on all sides except at the point where it is supported. Closely related to hanging shelves described on pages 99 to 102.

SWAG. Fabric draped in a looped effect suggestive of the fashion in which a garland of flowers might be hung. Elaborate top treatment for traditional window draperies.

185

SYMMETRICAL. Balance achieved by relying upon pairs of pieces evenly distributed around a dominating element such as a sofa. Matching tables, matching lamps, matching stools, or pull-up chairs set this way have a correct look that smacks of traditional formality. The principle may be applied to as modern a room as that below, but is more often seen in period settings.

SYNTHETIC. Artificial man-made substitute for a natural material. Ranges from rayons and leather-like plastics to plushy make-believe furs recently produced.

t

TABOURET. Type of stool, no longer sat upon, but serving as a table. Name derives from drum shape; can be made of metal, or porcelain in white or many colors.

TAMBOUR. Flexible door that slides along a groove following the curves of a chest. Made of thin strips of wood glued to canvas; is the roll of a rolltop desk.

TESTER. Framework that upholds the canopy on a four-poster bed. Evolved from the French word for head, this term expresses what a canopy does—it covers the head.

TÊTE-À-TÊTE. Nineteenth-century seat with chairs facing in opposite directions. Shaped curves give it a sinuous grace that put it back on the twentieth-century scene.

193

VICTORIAN. Era which took its name from the famed Queen of England whose purity of taste did not penetrate into the arts of decoration. Quite the contrary, it permitted a strange mixture of such unrelated objects as may be found in the two rooms illustrated here, both American interpretations of this English fashion.

207

VICTORIAN INFLUENCE. Flavor that pervades certain rooms today, which, while they do not duplicate the homes of our ancestors, preserve the traditions of chubby chairs, tiny tables, emphasis on bric-a-brac.

VITRINE. Cabinet of French origin that holds curios behind glass-enclosed shelves. For modern collectors, many are equipped with built-in lighting devices, the better to show up the encased precious objects.

WEDGWOOD. English pottery dating from the mid-eighteenth century, prominently associated with tasteful re-creations of classic urns and interesting innovations in wall, table, mantle, and door ornaments.

WALL-HUNG. Still another descriptive term to apply to suspended shelves—even a single one that serves as a telephone table.

WALL TREATMENTS. See page 216 and on.

WEBBING. Basket weave of burlap, at one time an undercover support for upholstery, now brought out in the open and used alone.

color schemes

Wall Treatments. Paper can add more than prettiness, sometimes lends itself to such architectural effects as that at left, where the border not only circles the striped walls but continues over the windows to take the place of a fabric swag. In the setting below, companion papers add interest. One is applied to the walls leading to the dining area, a second plainer plaid in mated colors covers a single wall of the room itself. Other walls are painted the lightest color while window shades match the paper.

Wall Treatments. Wood paneling for walls is subject to infinite variation, can be combined with walls not so treated, and goes particularly well with brick. In degrees of formality ranging from old weathered board taken from barns to the carved panelings of France (called *boiseries*), it can be finished in tones from dark teak and rosewood to the light pine hung in a chevron pattern behind the bed below. Either this or the walnut in the modern house at right provide quiet natural backgrounds against which to play bright color.

brighter colors

Wall Treatments. Fabric-covered walls, a time-honored device in traditional rooms, are putting in an appearance in those of more contemporary character. It looks more extravagant than it is. A simple wood frame can be made to fit the room, then the fabric is nailed to the frame and stretched tightly. In still simpler fashion, curtain rods, top and bottom, can hold the fabric in place, making it removable for cleaning. A traditional chintz, a modern bright red burlap used in the two rooms on these pages illustrate different effects that can be achieved. In the traditional dining room, paneling holds the fabric in place. The burlap is glued to the wall.

ACKNOWLEDGMENTS

Layouts designed by Arnold Hoffmann, Jr.

To the following group of manufacturers, importers, and shops, the author is grateful for photographic material supplied: B. Altman & Co., America House, A La Vieille Russie, Antique Art & Antique Dealers, Armstrong Cork Co., Artes de Mexico, Avard, Basic-Witz Furniture Industries, Baker Furniture Co., Bonniers, Yale Burge, Cabin Crafts, Celanese, Charak, Philip Colleck, Conso Trimming Co., Decorative Imports, Decorators Walk, De Gaal & Walker, Pino L. de Luca, Design Technics, Drexel, Dunbar, Dupal Furniture Co., Foam Latex Rubber Council, French & Co., Ginsberg & Levy, Gorham, Hammacher Schlemmer, Hitchcock Chair Co., House of Spain, Georg Jensen, Edwin Jackson, Herman Kashins, Kittinger, Knoll Associates, Lane Furniture Co., Arthur H. Lee, Macy's, Morrison Imports, Palladio, Paper Plate and Container Institute, Phillips Galleries, Piazza, Harvey Probber, Raymor, Lew Raynes, Royal System, Isabel Scott, James Seeman Studios, Selig, Spanish Trading Center, Sprague & Carleton, W. & J. Sloane, Stockwell Wallpaper Co., David Stockwell, Steuben, John Strauss, Syroco, Tomlinson, Tropi-cal, Thonet, U.S. Plywood, U.S. Rubber, V'Soske, Otto M. Wasserman, Wedgwood.

Appreciation should also be expressed for the cooperation of the interior designers listed below whose work is included in the following pages: Beryl Austrian, Leigh Allen, David Barrett, Braswell-Cook, Baldwin & Machado, John Bedenkapp, Samson Berman, David Eugene Bell, Everett Brown, Alexander Calder, d'Argout Ferguson, Marion Dorn, Mary Dunn, Charles Eames, Eddie Fredericks, Lawrence Fleischman, Augusta Gassner, Alexander Girard, Jeremiah Goodman, Hector Grant, Henriette Granville, Michael Greer, Jack Hartrick, Patricia Harvey, Marjorie Boradaille Helsel, Albert Herbert, Joseph Hoffman, Evelyn Jablow, Vladimir Kagan, Melanie Kahane, John Keal, Virginia Kelly, Paul Krauss, Charles & Camille Lehman, Robert Lindenthal, George Lippart, Alvin Lustig, Jack Macurdy, Jerome Manashaw, Harry Martin, William Parker McFadden, Ed Motyka, Muller-Bachich, Robert Luther Myers, George Nagashima, George Nelson, Geraldine Nicosia, Bengt Nordquist, William Pahlmann, Gary Pizzarelli, Leonard H. Price, Gio Ponti, William Raiser, T. H. Robsjohn Gibbings, Howard Rothberg Perry, Renny Salzman, Astrid Sampe, Harold Schwartz, Staniford Squire, Mrs. Belmont Tobin, Mies van der Rohe, John Van Koert, Robert Walker, Craig Weston, David Whitcomb, John Wisner, Edward Wormley, Tom Yee, May Veronica Yhap.

Also assisting were a group of galleries, museums, and individual artists. They are: American Craftsmen Council, Asia Society, Brooklyn Museum, Henry Ford Museum, Norman LaLiberte, Metropolitan Museum of Art, Mondrian, Museum of American Indian, Julian Stanczak, Stony Point Folk Art Gallery, Bjorn Wiinblad, Winterthur Museum, Tapio Wirkkala.

Also helpful in the compilation of this material were the members of my own staff: Gladys Gough and Michael Landers.